SPIDER COLORING BOOK

CRYSTAL COLORING BOOKS

Copyright © 2019 Crystal Coloring Books
All rights reserved.

ISBN: 9781705355039

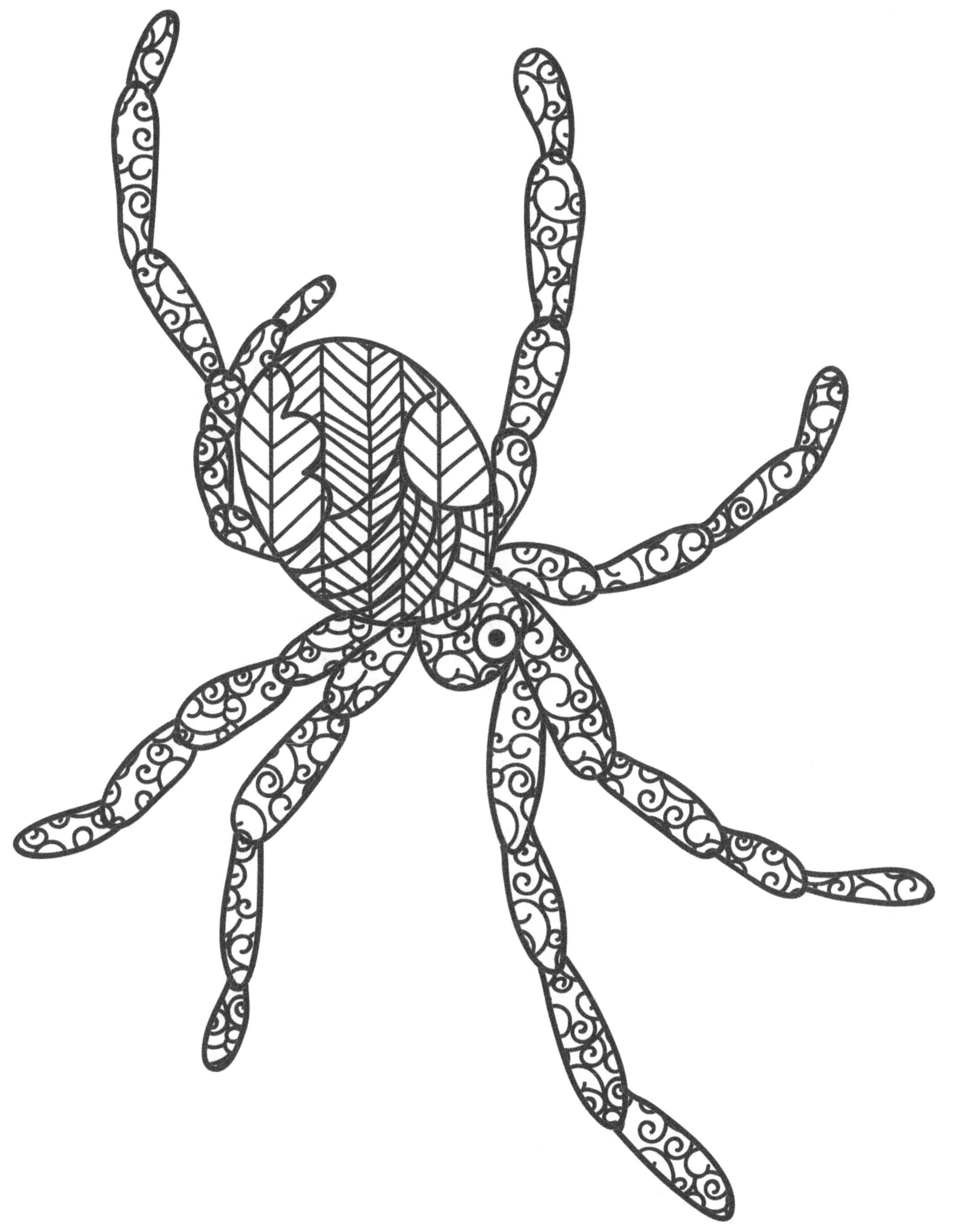

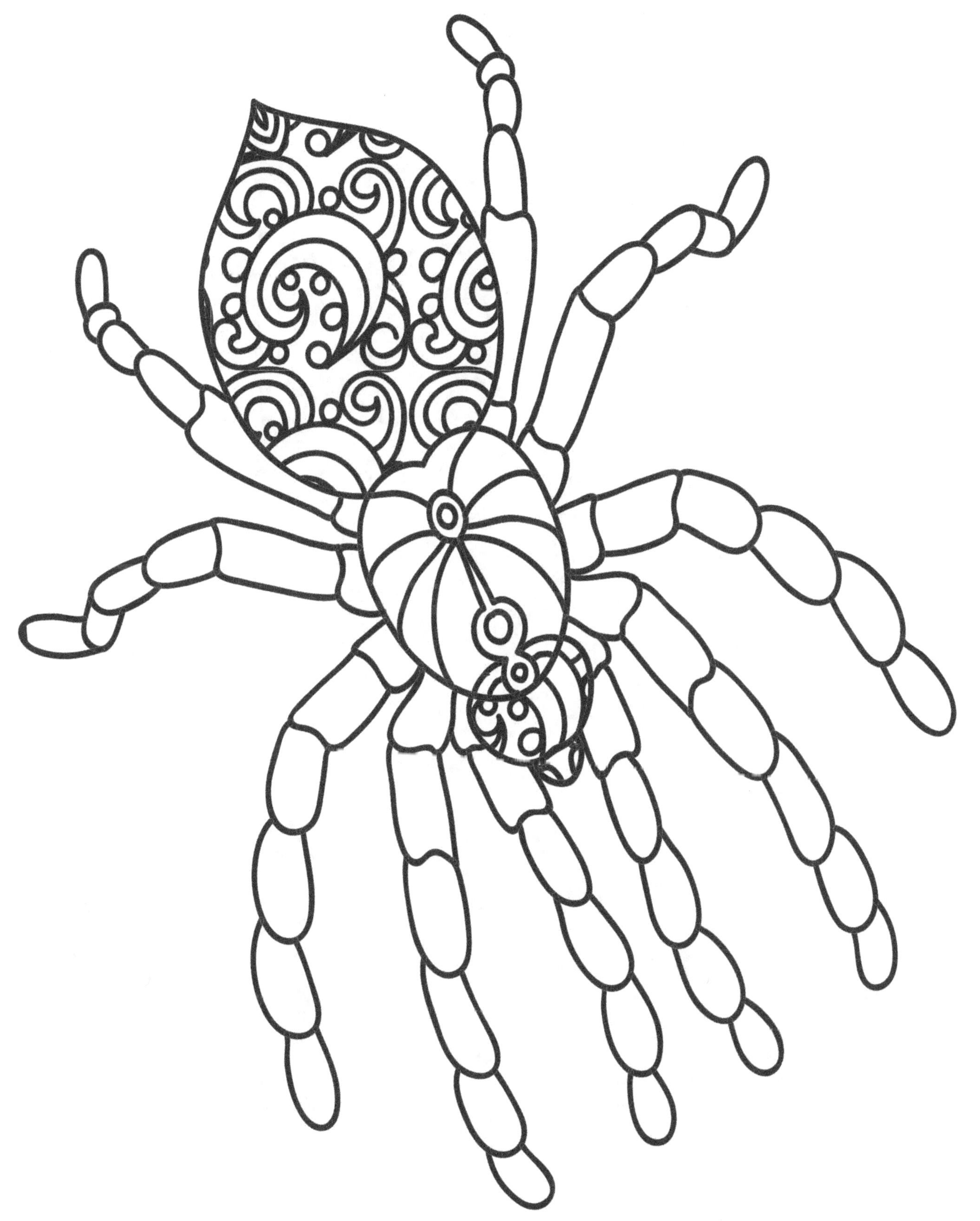

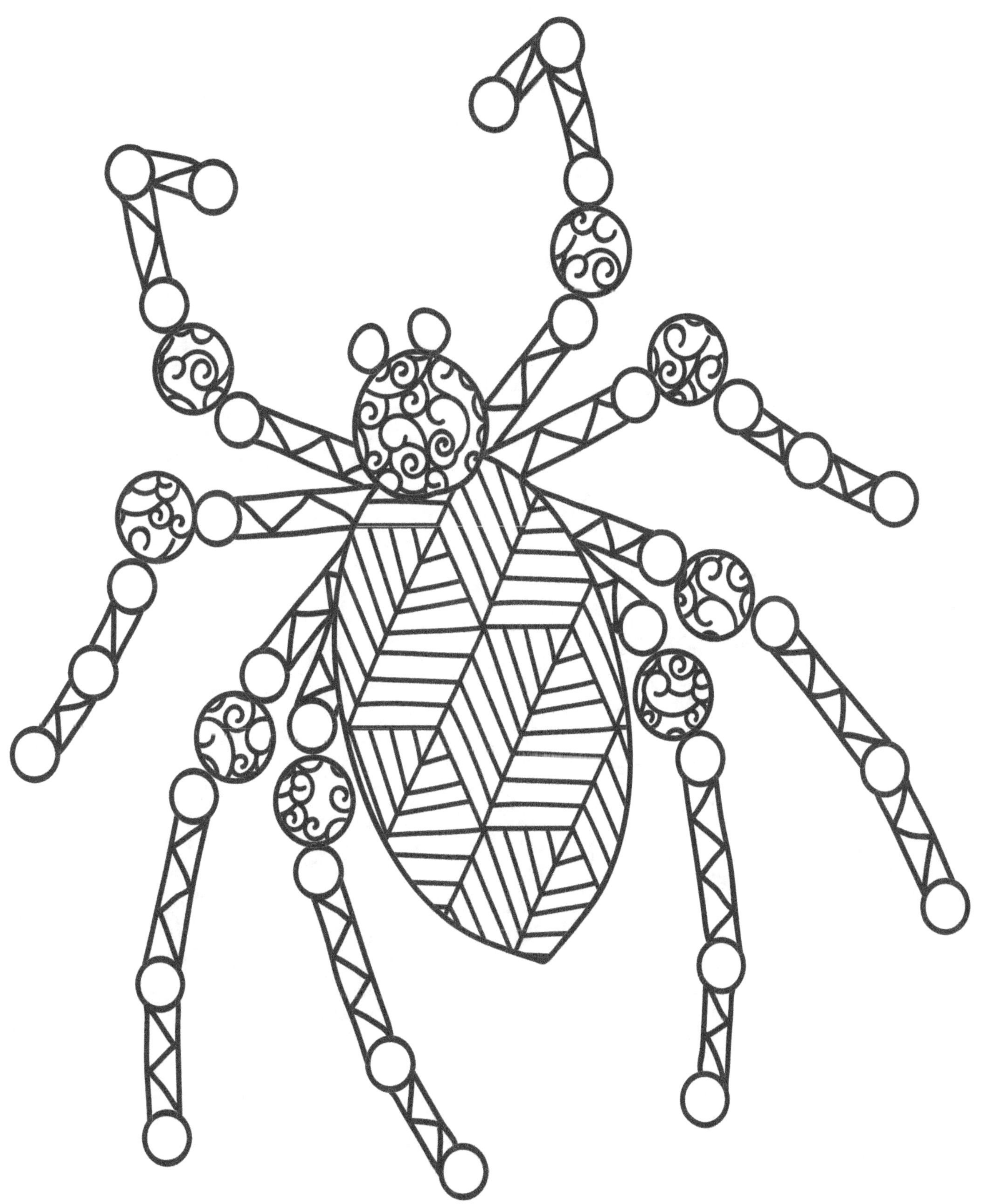

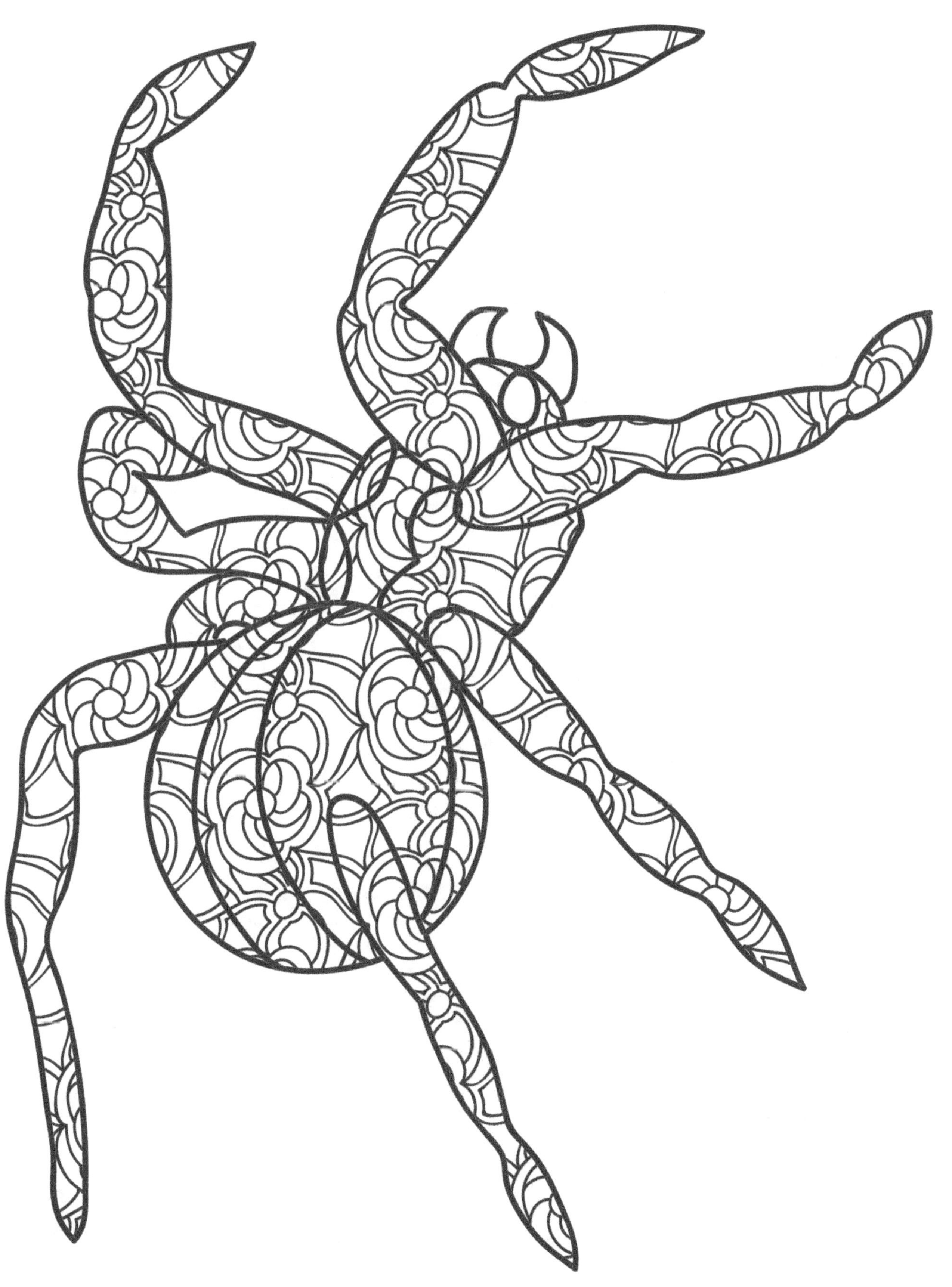

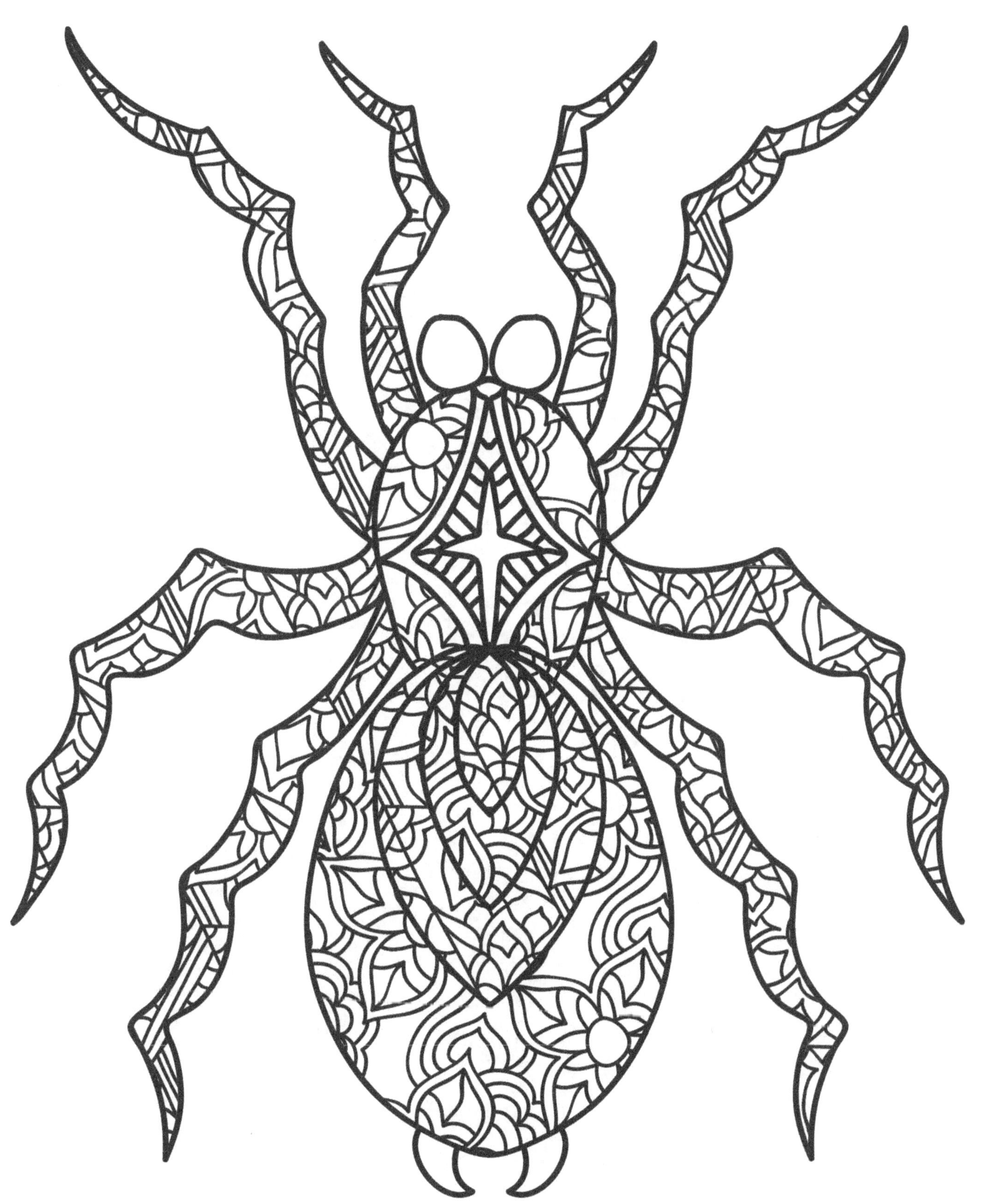

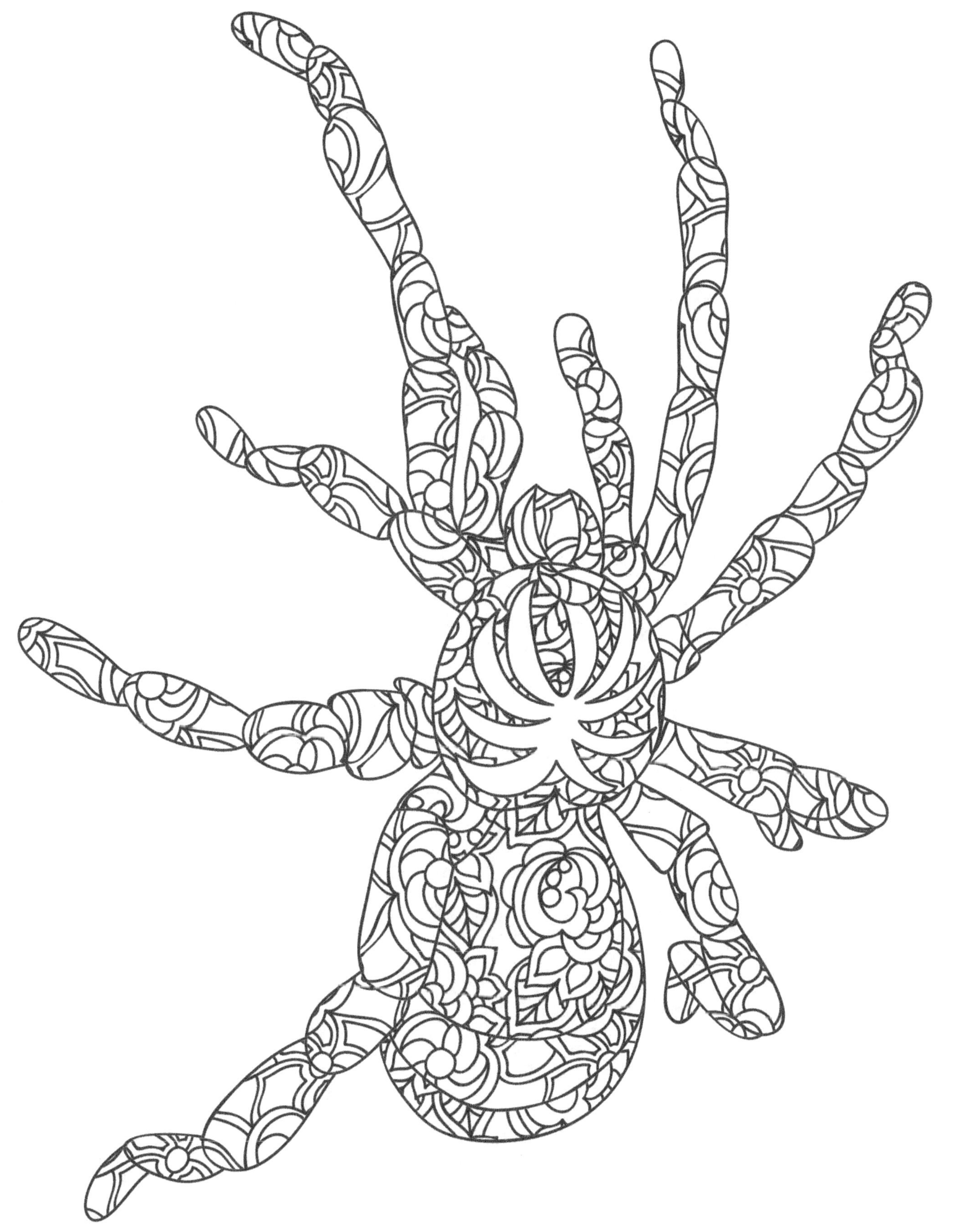

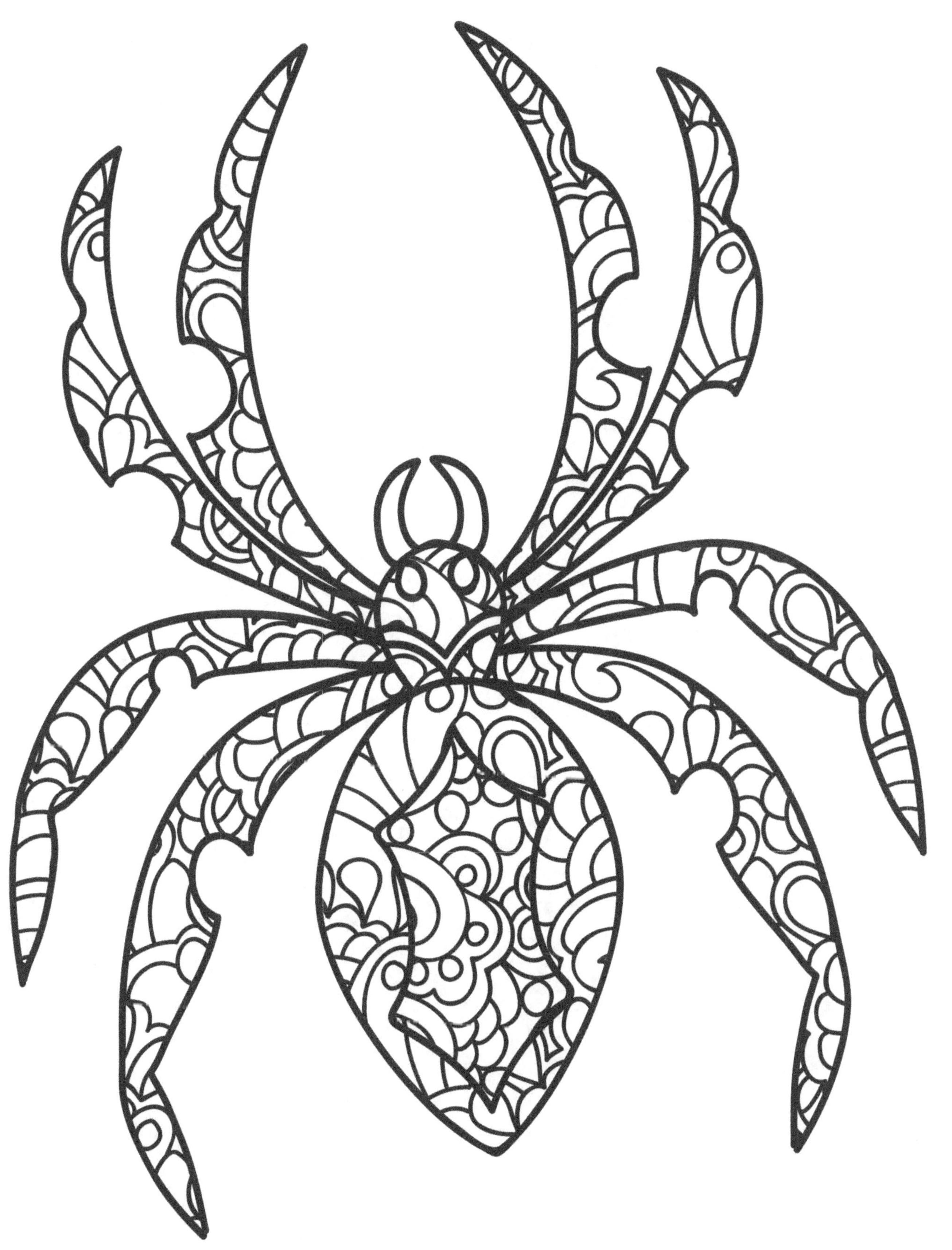

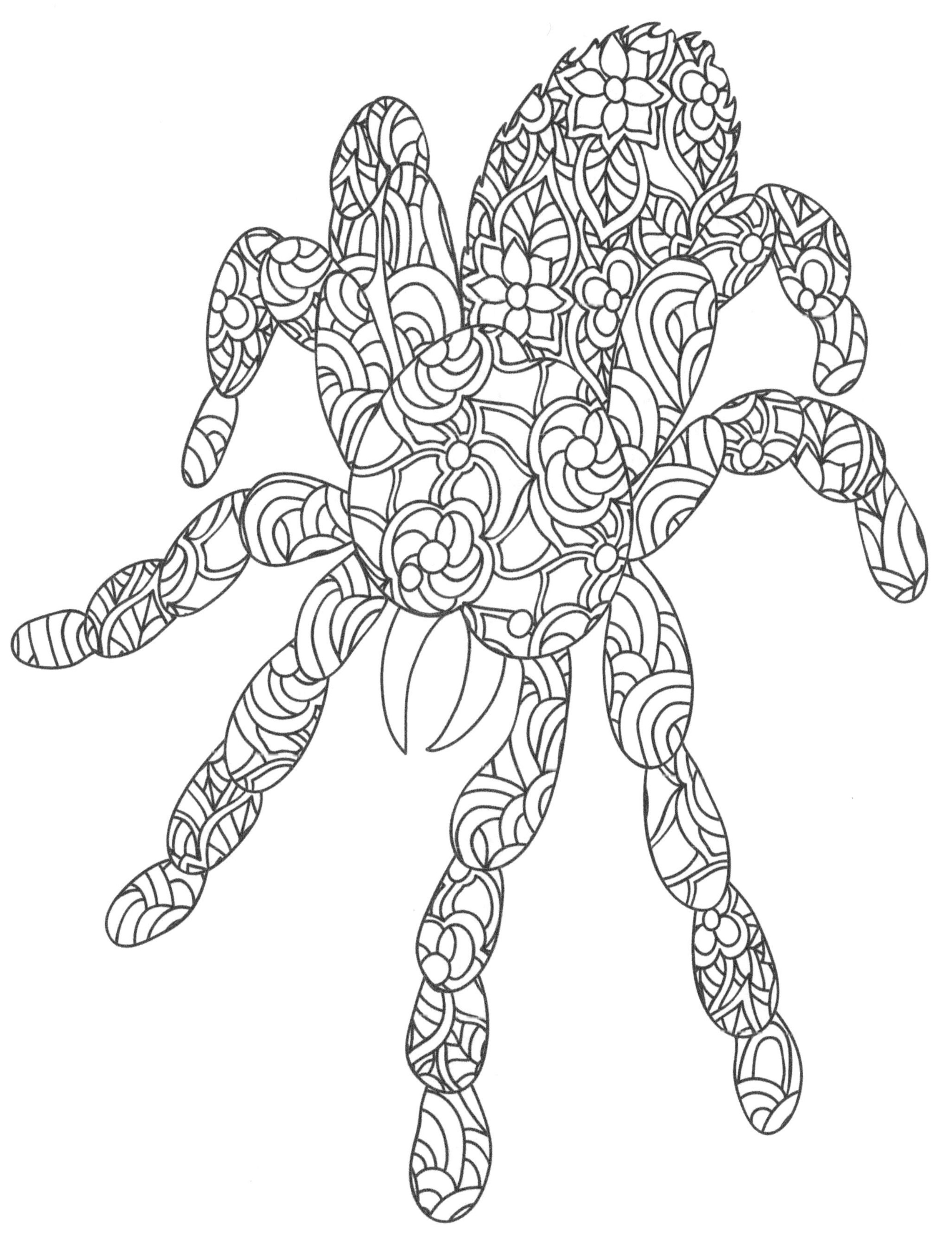

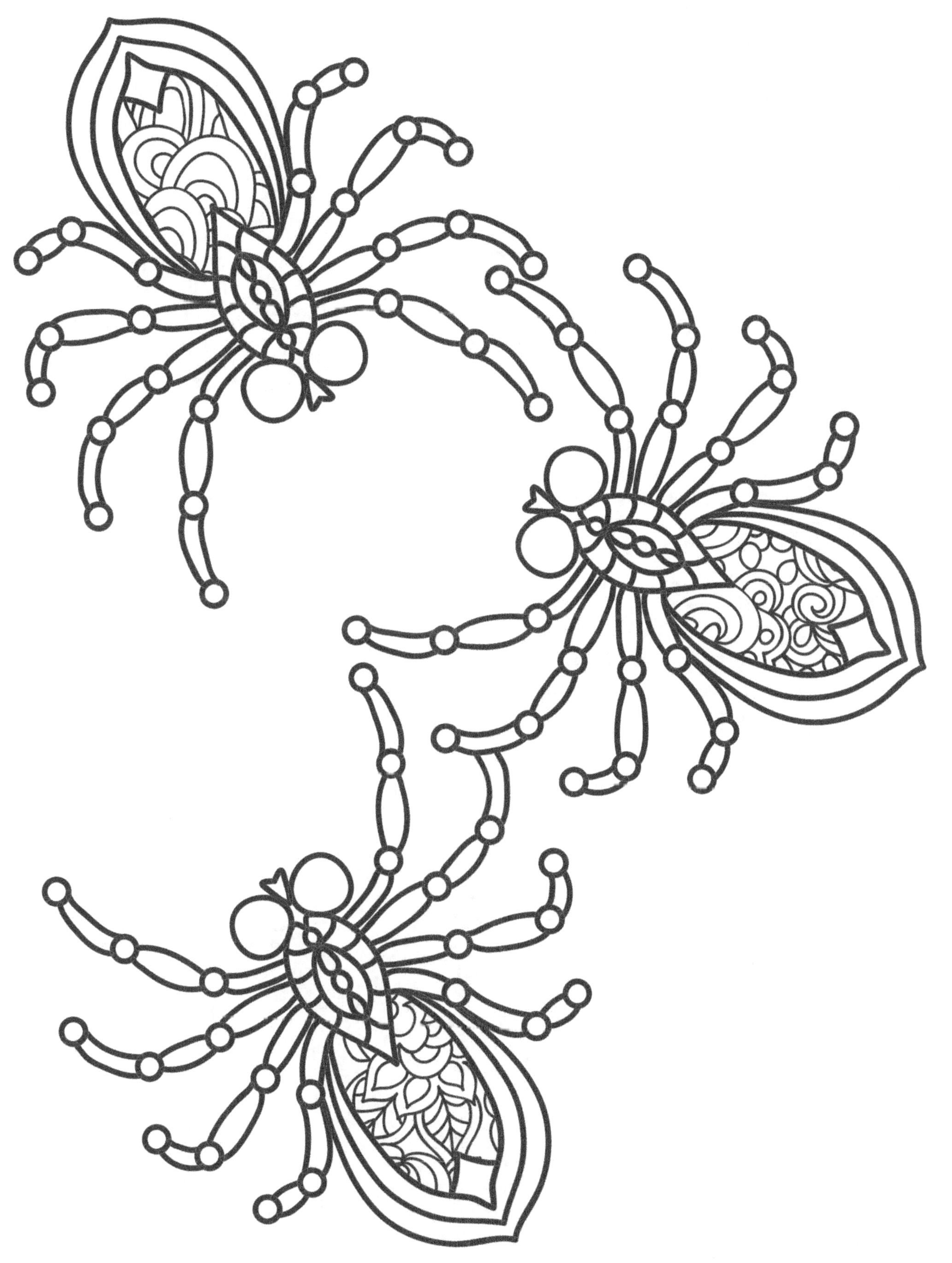

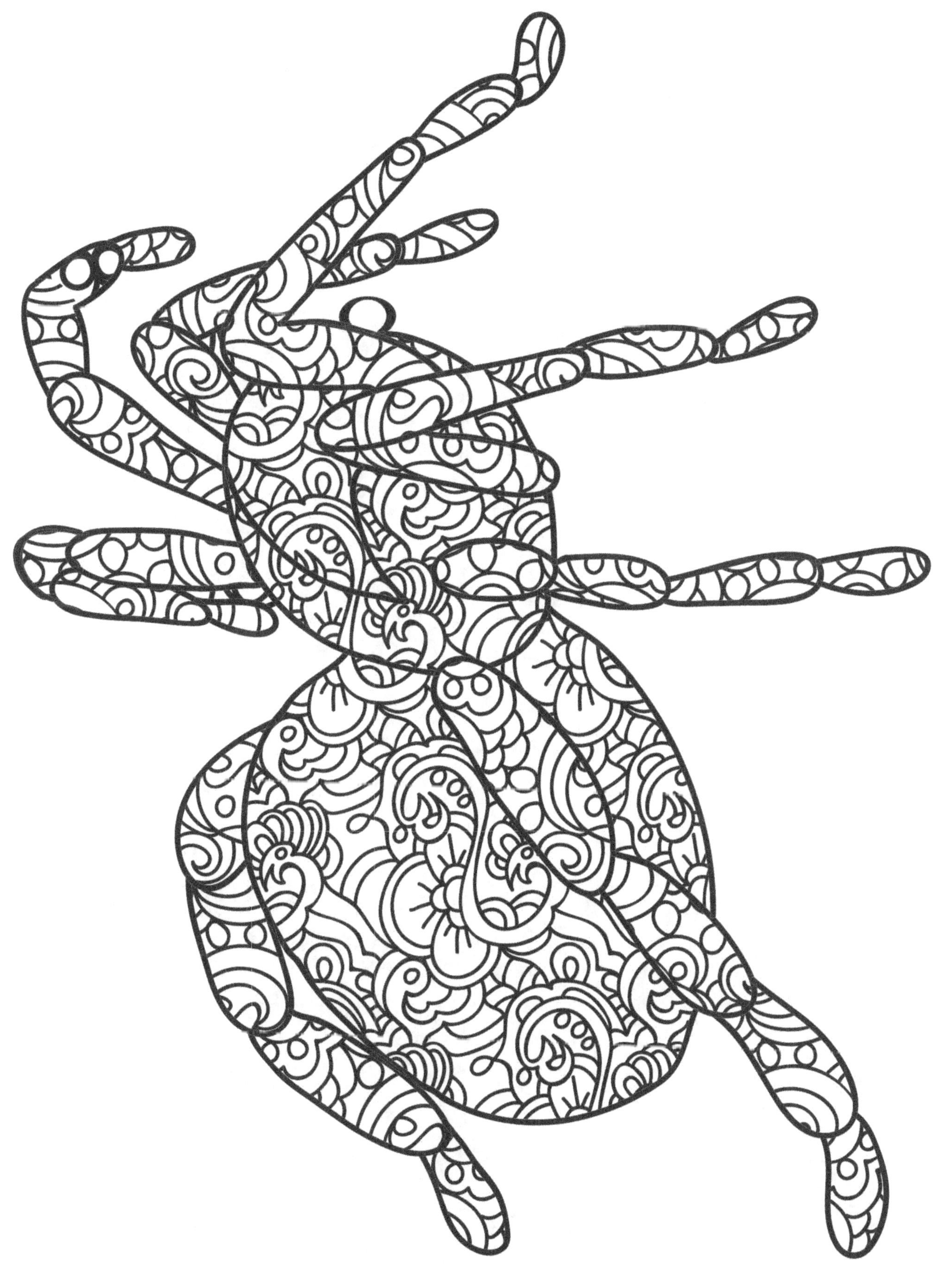

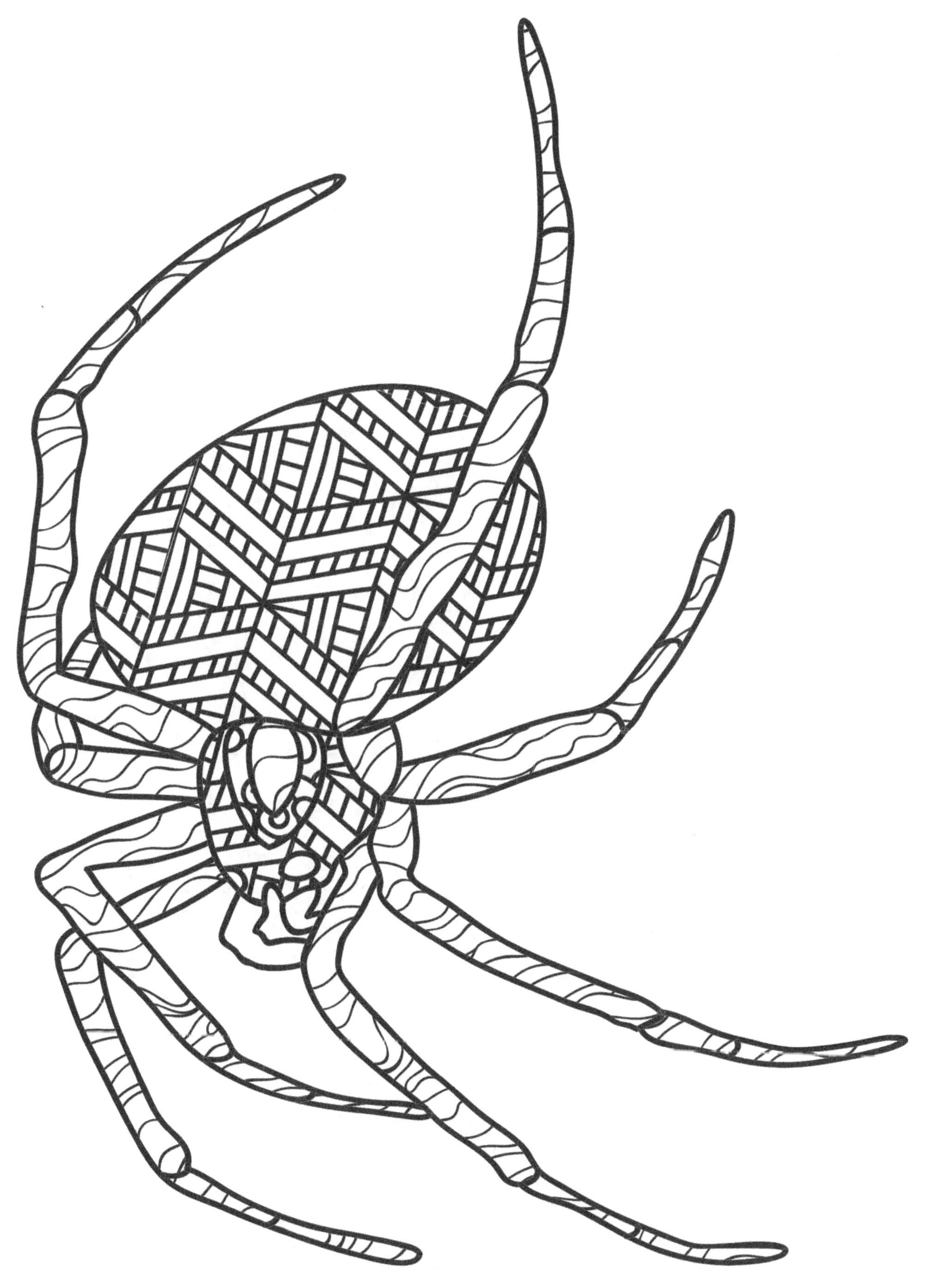

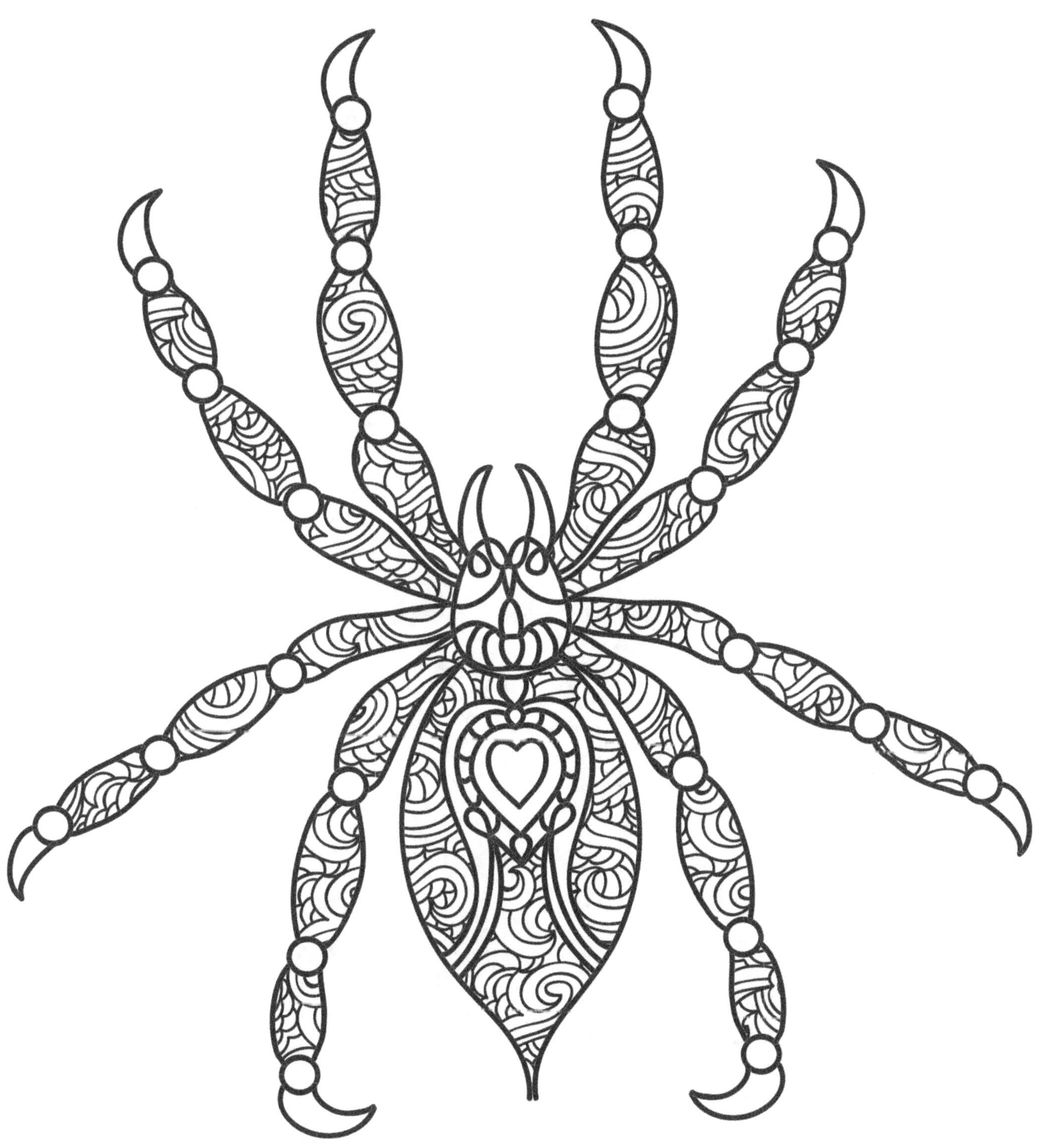

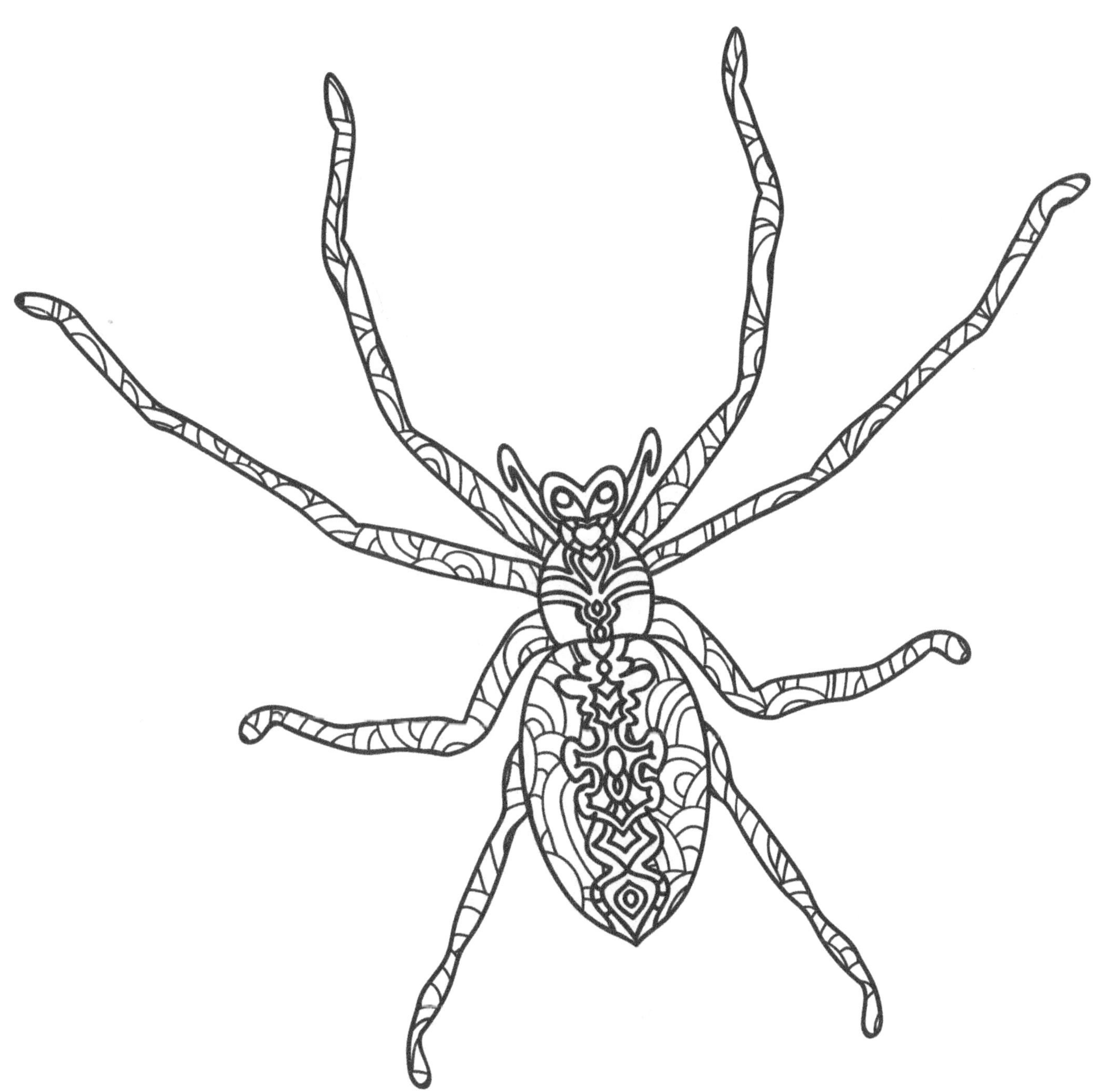

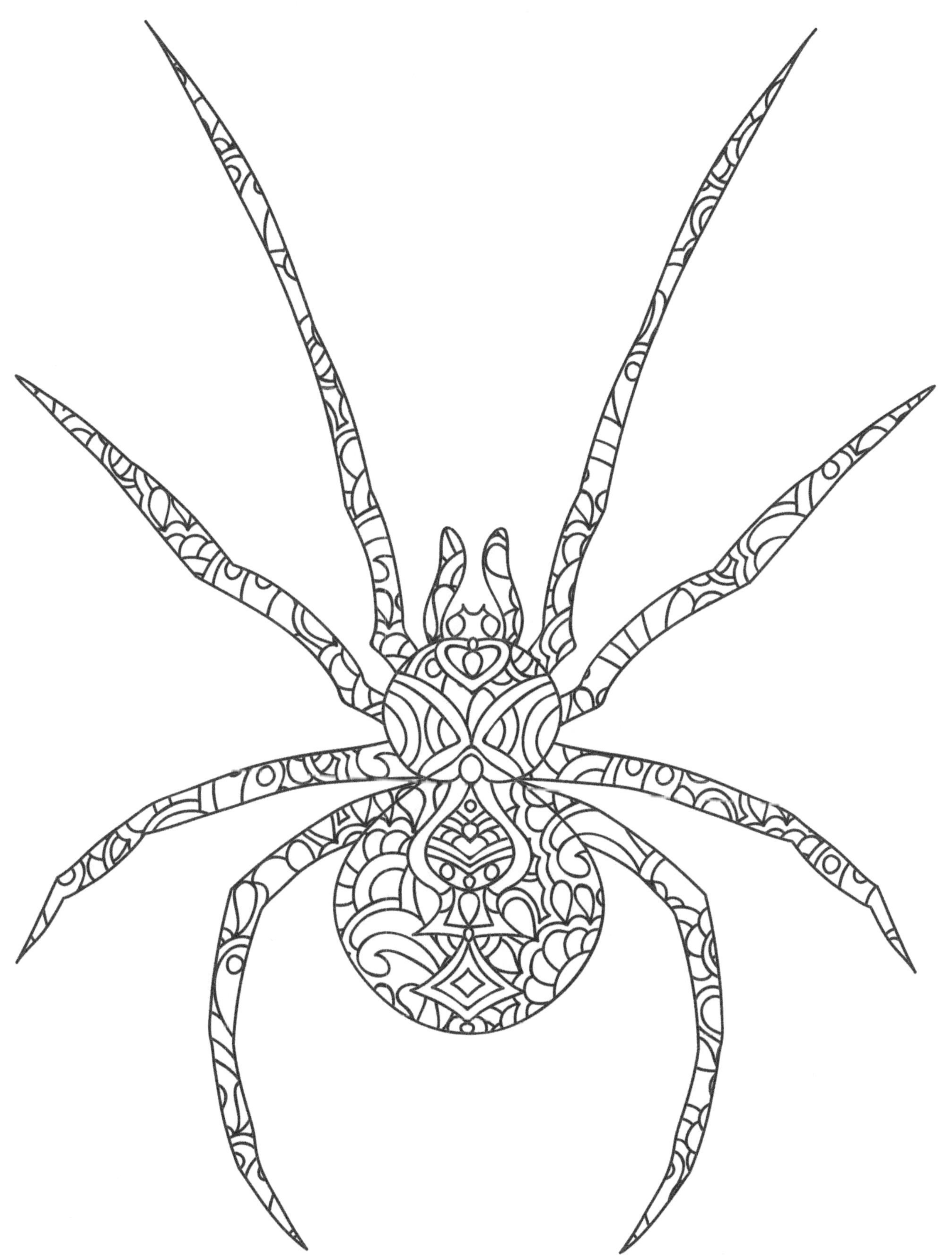

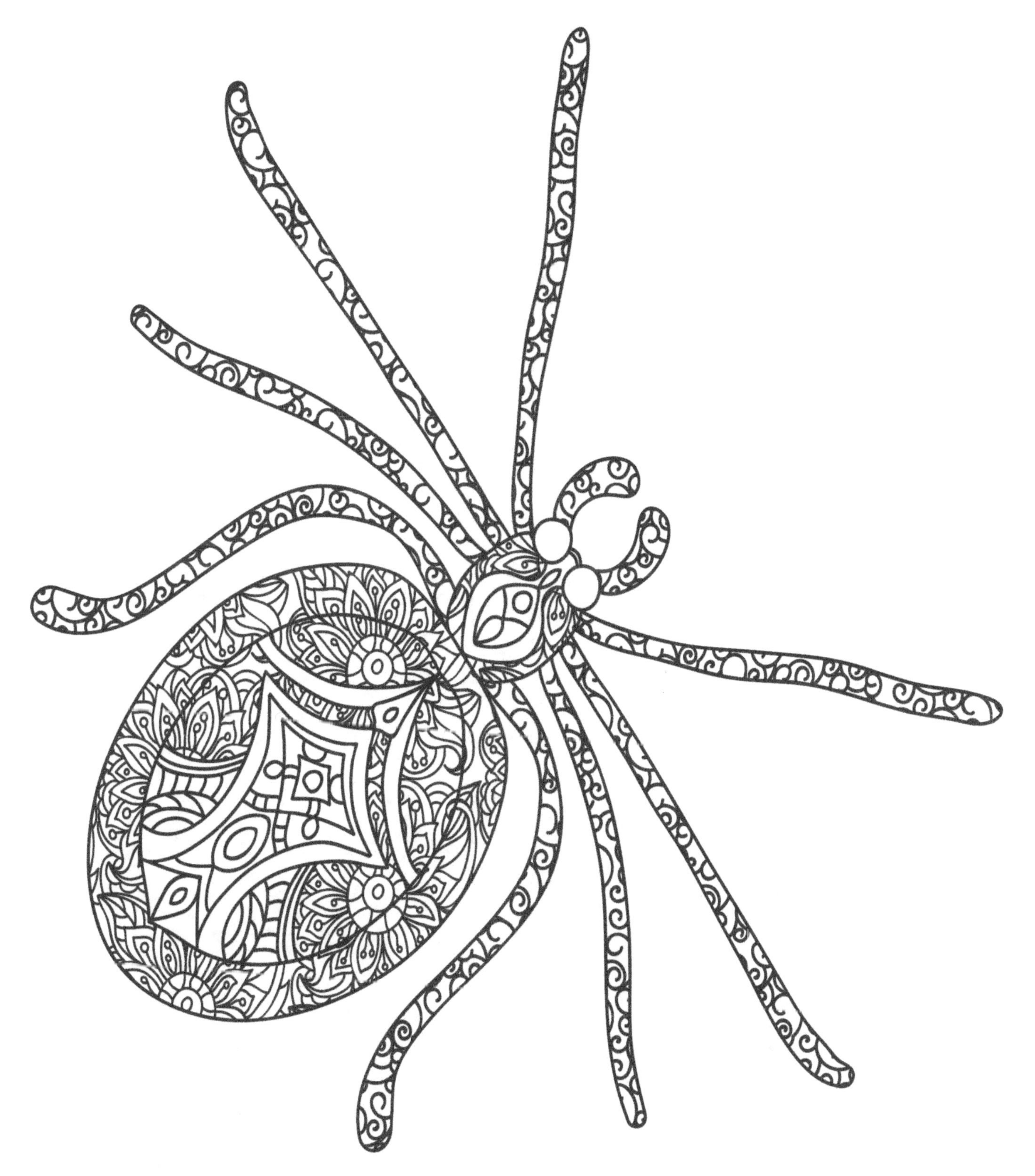

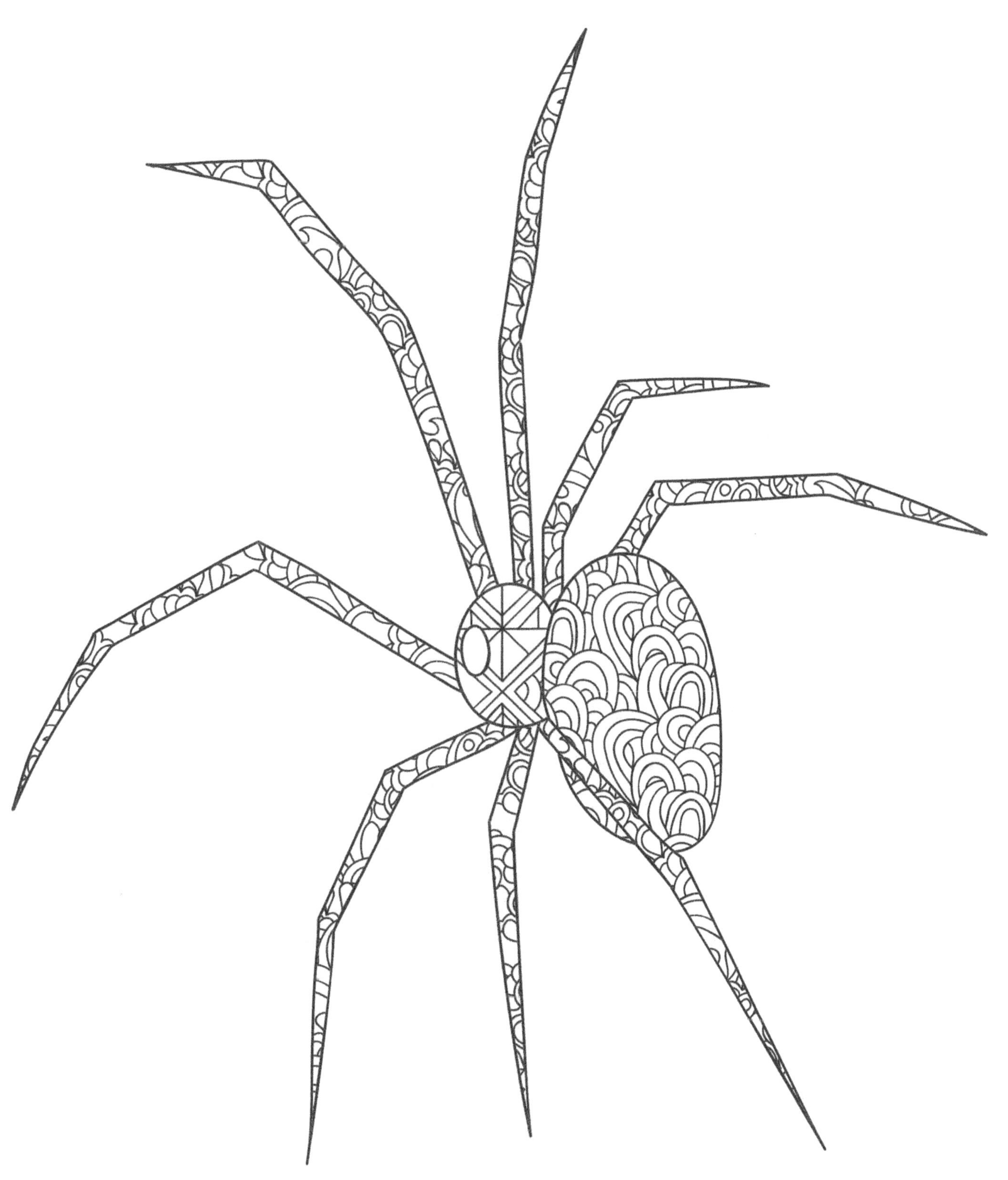

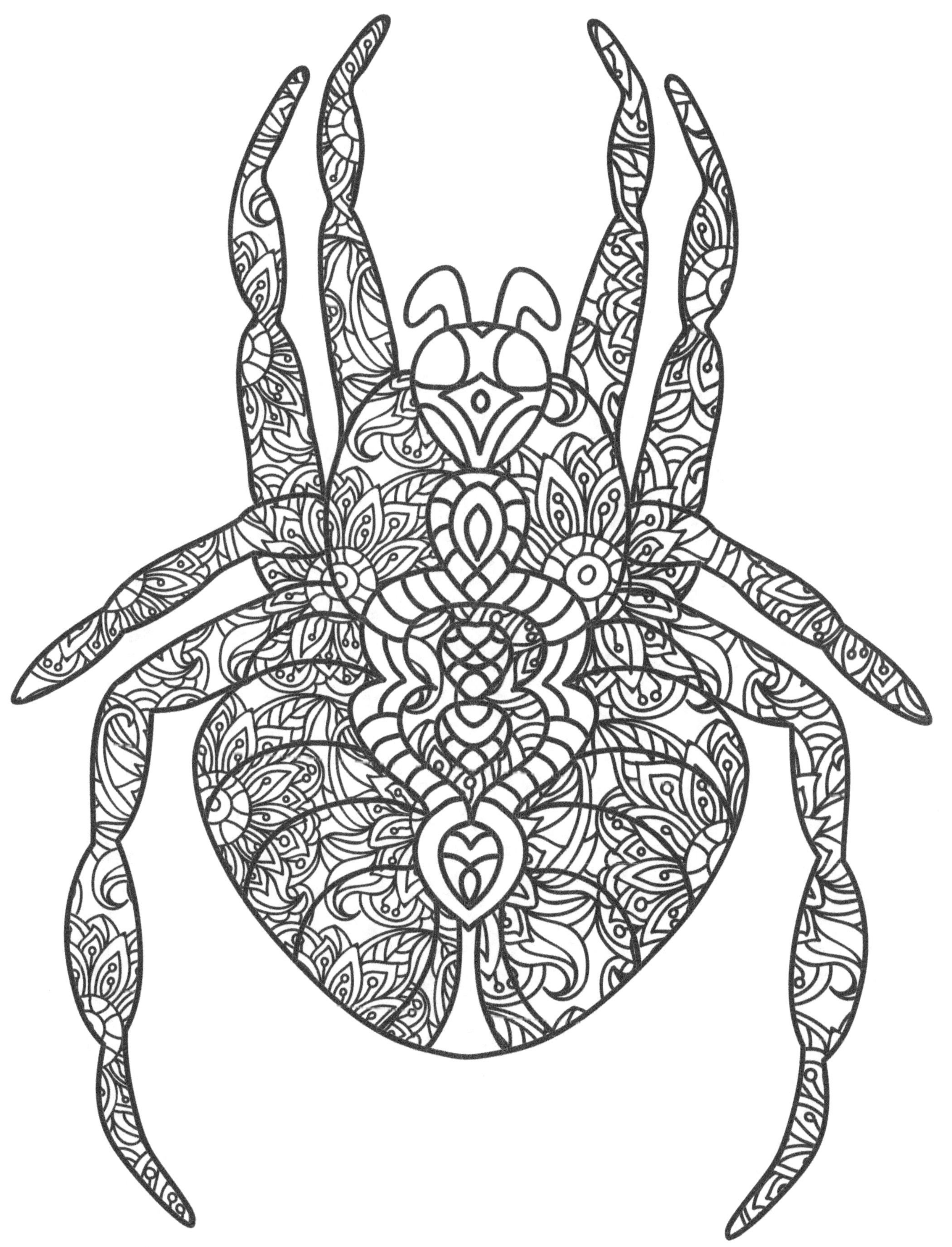

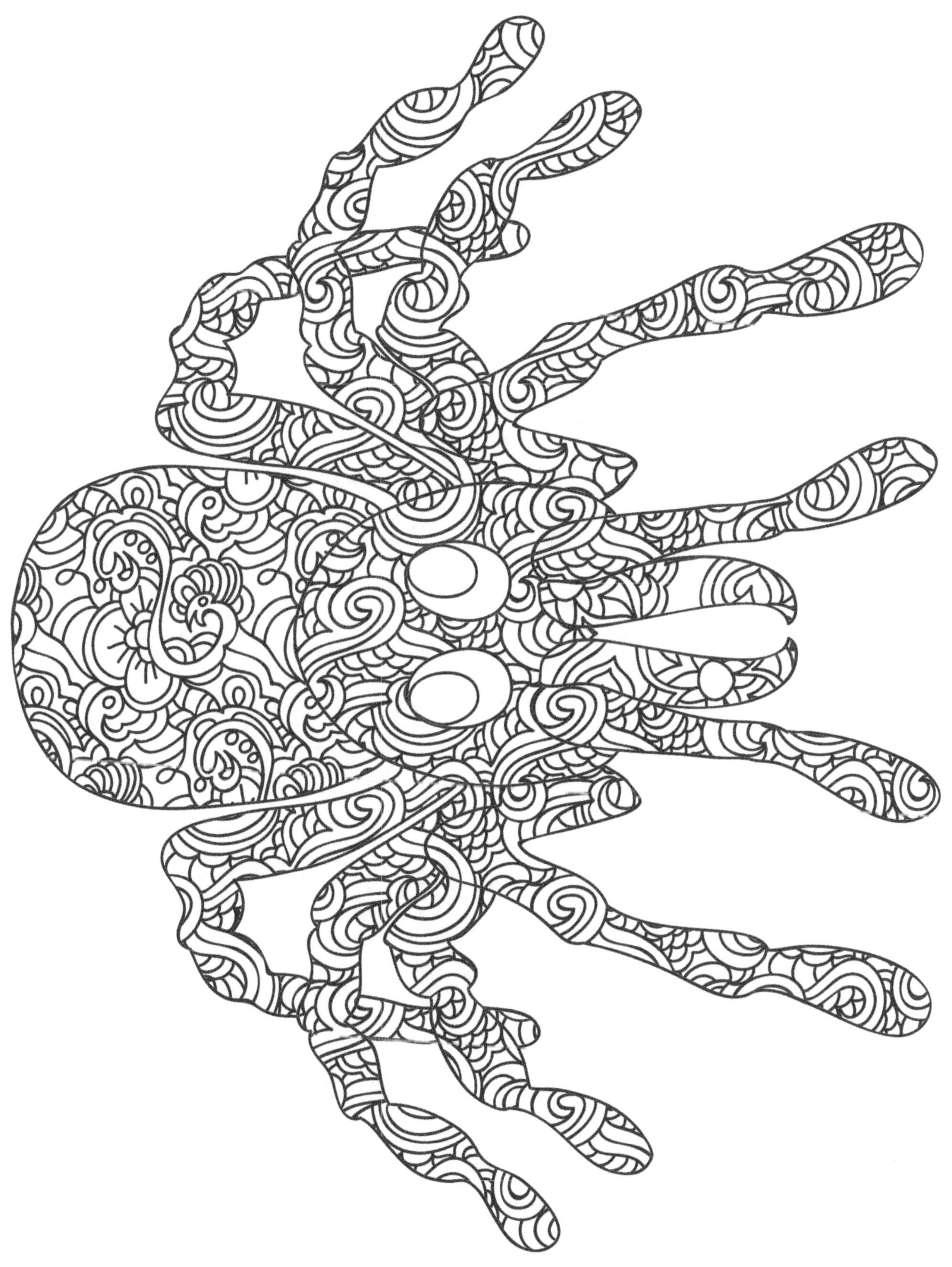

COLOR TEST PAGE

COLOR TEST PAGE

www.ingramcontent.com/pod-product-compliance
Lightning Source LLC
Chambersburg PA
CBHW081559270726
48657CB00029B/3395